100 BIBLE QUIZZES

Activity Book

100 Bible Quizzes Activity Book

Bible Pathway Adventures® is a trademark of BPA Publishing Ltd.
Defenders of the Faith® is a trademark of BPA Publishing Ltd.

ISBN: 978-1-98-858554-3

Author: Pip Reid
Creative Director: Curtis Reid

For free Bible resources including coloring pages, worksheets, puzzles and more, visit our website at:

www.biblepathwayadventures.com

◇◇ INTRODUCTION ◇◇

How old was Noah when the flood began? Who betrayed Yeshua for 30 pieces of silver? Increase your Bible knowledge with our *100 Bible Quizzes Activity Book*! Packed with a mix of engaging Bible quizzes to help you learn about the people, places, and events of the Bible. Includes detailed scripture references for further Bible reading and a handy answer key for educators. The perfect discipleship resource for Bible study groups, Homeschoolers, Sabbath and Sunday School teachers, and families.

Bible Pathway Adventures® helps educators teach children a Biblical faith in a fun and creative way. We do this via our Activity Books and free printable activities – available on our website: www.biblepathwayadventures.com

Thanks for buying this Activity Book and supporting our ministry. Every book purchased helps us continue our work providing free Classroom Packs and discipleship resources to families and missions everywhere.

The search for Truth is more fun than Tradition!

◆◇ TABLE OF CONTENTS ◇◆

Take a trip back in time

Our vision is to provide culturally, historically, and biblically sound materials to help you teach your children a Biblical faith. When we read the Bible in the context of the ancient Hebrew culture, it comes alive and unlocks the beauty and depth of the Scriptures.

Why do we sometimes use Hebrew names like Yeshua? Or include the Biblical Feasts like the Feast of Unleavened Bread and Shavu'ot (Pentecost)? Because understanding these Hebrew names and festivals helps us unlock the richness of the Biblical account – a richness and understanding that can get lost when only seen from a modern Western perspective.

For example, Matthew 26:34 says… "Before the rooster crows, you will deny me three times." In its cultural and historical context, this was not actually a rooster crowing but the Temple Crier, a priest who announced the morning Temple services and sacrifices at the time of Yeshua. Did you know the modern English name of 'Jesus' has only been used for 500 years? This means Mary and the disciples would have called the Messiah by His actual Hebrew name, Yeshua or Yehoshua, which means, 'God saves,' or 'God is my salvation.'

So…let's take a trip back in time and enjoy the richness of the Bible!

The CREATION

Read Genesis 1-2. Answer the questions below.

1. What did God call the light?

2. What was created on the second day?

3. What did God call dry land?

4. What is the name of the light that rules the day?

5. On what day did God create swimming creatures?

6. In what image did God create men and women?

7. On which day did God rest?

8. How did God water the earth?

9. How did God create a man?

10. How did God create a woman?

ADAM & EVE

Read Genesis 2-5. Answer the questions below.

1. In the beginning, how did God water the earth?

2. Where did God plant a garden?

3. Why was Adam put in the garden?

4. Who named all the birds and animals?

5. Why did Adam name his wife Eve?

6. Who first ate fruit from the tree of knowledge of good and evil?

7. After Adam and Eve saw they were naked, what did they do?

8. Where did God send them after they ate from the tree of knowledge?

9. What were the names of Adam and Eve's first two sons?

10. How old was Adam when he died?

Garden of EDEN

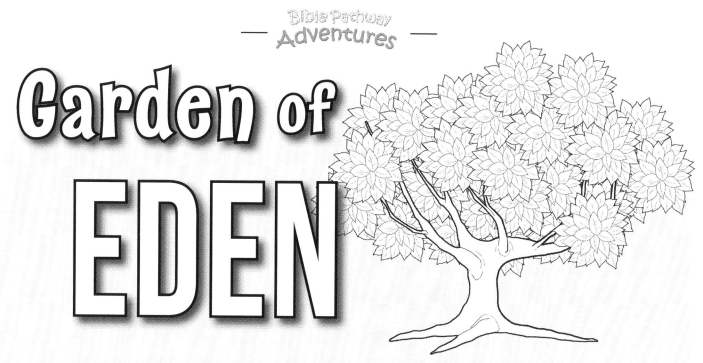

Read Genesis 2-3. Answer the questions below.

1. Where did God plant a garden?

2. What was the name of the first river that flowed out of the garden?

3. What metal was found in Havilah?

4. What stones were found in Havilah?

5. What was the name of the fourth river that flowed out of the garden?

6. What river flowed around the land of Cush?

7. From which tree did God forbid Adam to eat its fruit?

8. What happened after God caused Adam to sleep?

9. What did the serpent say to Eve?

10. What did God place at the east of the garden to keep Adam and Eve out?

CAIN & ABEL

Read Genesis 4. Answer the questions below.

1. Who was Eve's first-born son?

2. What was Cain's job?

3. What was Abel's job?

4. What did Cain offer for a sacrifice?

5. Why did Cain become angry?

6. What did Cain do to Abel?

7. Who lied to God when he was asked where his brother was?

8. Because Cain murdered Abel, how did God curse him?

9. Who was Cain and Abel's father?

10. After Cain fled from God, in which land did he settle?

Noah's ARK

Read Genesis 6-8. Answer the questions below.

1. Who was Noah's father?

2. How long was Noah's ark?

3. What material was Noah's ark made from?

4. How many windows did the ark have?

5. How many pairs of each 'clean' animal did Noah take on the ark?

6. How old was Noah when the Flood started?

7. What did the dove bring back to Noah?

8. On which mountain range did Noah's ark rest?

9. What did Noah build when he came out of the ark?

10. What was the sign of a covenant between God and Noah?

Tower of BABEL

Read Genesis 11:1-9. Answer the questions below.

1. Why was it easy for people to work together to build the tower of Babel?

2. How high did they plan to build the tower?

3. What materials did people use to build the tower?

4. Who came down to see the tower?

5. How did Yahweh stop their work?

6. Why did the people stop building the tower?

7. What was the name of the place where they tried to build the tower?

8. What happened to the people after they stopped building the tower?

9. What did the people think the tower would protect them from?

10. Where is the modern-day land of Shinar?

ABRAHAM

Read Genesis 12:1-20, 14:1-15:20, 17:1-27, and 21:1-34. Answer the questions below.

1. Where was Abram born?

2. Who was Abram's father?

3. Who did Abram marry?

4. Which land did God promise to Abram?

5. What did Abram do after Lot was taken prisoner?

6. What did Melchizedek give to Abram?

7. What did God's new name for Abram mean?

8. How old was Abraham when he became a father?

9. What was the name of Abraham's special son?

10. To which land did Abraham travel to escape the famine?

Lot's
ESCAPE

Read Genesis 18-19. Answer the questions below.

1. Where did God tell Abraham he would destroy Sodom and Gomorrah?

2. What relation was Lot to Abraham?

3. How many angels visited Sodom?

4. What type of bread did Lot give the angels?

5. What happened to the men who demanded Lot hand over his guests?

6. Who did not believe Lot when he told them that Sodom would be destroyed?

7. What rained down on Sodom and Gomorrah?

8. What did the angels say to Lot as he fled the city?

9. What happened to Lot's wife when she looked back at the city?

10. Where did Lot and his daughters go to after leaving Sodom?

Birth of ISAAC

Read Genesis 18:1-21:34. Answer the questions below.

1 How many men visited Abraham at the oaks of Mamre?

2 How did Abraham welcome the men?

3 What was the name of Abraham's wife?

4 What important message did the three men give Abraham?

5 How did Abraham's wife react when she heard the message?

6 How old was Abraham when his son was born?

7 What did Abraham name his son?

8 After how many days was Abraham's son circumcized?

9 How did Abraham and Sarah celebrate their son's weaning?

10 Why did Abraham take his son to the land of Moriah?

ISAAC & REBEKAH

Read Genesis 24:1-67. Answer the questions below.

1. Who was the father of Isaac?

2. Where did Abraham send his servant to find a wife for Isaac?

3. How many camels did the servant take with him?

4. Where did the servant find Rebekah?

5. What jewelry did the servant give Rebekah?

6. What was the name of Rebekah's father?

7. What did Rebekah do when she first saw Isaac?

8. How old was Isaac when he married Rebekah?

9. Where did Isaac and Rebekah live after they were married?

10. What were the names of Isaac and Rebekah's two sons?

JACOB & ESAU

Read Genesis 25:19-34. Answer the questions below.

1. Who was Jacob and Esau's mother?

2. Who was Jacob and Esau's father?

3. God said Jacob and Esau were what in the womb?

4. How did God describe Esau?

5. Which son did Rebekah love the most?

6. For what did Esau sell his birthright to Jacob?

7. What was Esau doing while Jacob stole his birthright blessing?

8. What did Esau want to do after Jacob 'stole' the birthright blessing?

9. How did Jacob fool Isaac into thinking he was Esau?

10. Who was Jacob's first wife?

JACOB

Read Genesis 25:19–50:14.
Answer the questions below.

1. Who was Jacob's mother?

2. From which land did Isaac tell Jacob not to take a wife?

3. Who was Jacob's grandfather?

4. What did Jacob see in his dream at Bethel?

5. Who was Jacob's first wife?

6. How many sons did Jacob (Israel) have?

7. What new name did God give Jacob?

8. Who was Jacob's favorite son?

9. Why did Jacob and his family move to Egypt?

10. How old was Jacob when he died?

JOSEPH

Read Genesis 37:1-36, 39:1-32, 40:1-44:34, and 46:1-34. Answer the questions below.

1. What was the name of Joseph's father?
2. What was Joseph's first dream?
3. How did Joseph's brothers get rid of him?
4. What was the name of Joseph's master in Egypt?
5. Whose dreams in prison did Joseph understand?
6. What did Joseph do for Pharaoh?
7. Why did Jacob send his sons to Egypt?
8. What did Joseph tell his servant to hide in Benjamin's sack?
9. What were the names of Joseph's two sons?
10. Where did Joseph's family live after they moved to Egypt?

MOSES

Read Exodus 2:1-13:36. Answer the questions below.

1. Moses was of which tribe of Israel?

2. Who found Moses in a basket by the river?

3. What was the name of Moses' brother?

4. After Moses killed an Egyptian, where did he go?

5. How did the Angel of God appear to Moses when he was a shepherd?

6. Who was Moses' wife?

7. What did Moses do in the wilderness for forty years?

8. What did Moses toss into the air to start the sixth plague?

9. To escape the final plague, what instructions did Moses give the Hebrews?

10. From which land did Moses help the Hebrews escape?

The burning BUSH

Read Exodus 3:1-4:31. Answer the questions below.

1) Where did Moses see the burning bush?

2) What did God tell Moses to remove?

3) Who did God say He was?

4) What did Moses do when God told him who He was?

5) What instructions did God give Moses?

6) What two signs did God give Moses?

7) What did Moses tell God he could not do well?

8) Who did God give Moses to help him speak to Pharaoh?

9) After speaking with God, who did Moses go and see?

10) What did God promise the Egyptians would give the Israelites when they left Egypt?

Ten plagues of EGYPT

Read Exodus 7:14-13:16. Answer the questions below.

1. What was the first plague?

2. Egyptian magicians were able to copy which plagues?

3. What was the fourth plague?

4. Ashes were used in which plague?

5. What was the ninth plague?

6. What was the last plague?

7. How many plagues did God send on Egypt?

8. Who hardened Pharaoh's heart so he wouldn't free the Hebrews?

9. Whose bones did Moses take with him when he left Egypt?

10. The Hebrews left Egypt during which Appointed Time (Feast)?

The Passover MEAL

Read Exodus 12:1-32, Matthew 1:1-16, and Mark 15:1-22.
Answer the questions below.

1. How many plagues did God send on Egypt?

2. How did the Hebrews protect themselves from the final plague?

3. On what day of the month did God tell the Hebrews to find a Passover lamb?

4. On what day on the month were the Hebrews told to kill their Passover lamb?

5. What food did Yah tell the Israelites to eat for the Passover meal?

6. What type of bread did the Israelites take with them when they left Egypt?

7. The Passover meal takes place at the start of which Appointed Time?

8. How long were the Israelites told to observe this meal?

9. Where was Yeshua crucified?

10. Yeshua was of which tribe of Israel?

Red Sea CROSSING

Read Exodus 14:1-31. Answer the questions below.

1. Who led the Israelites out of Egypt?

2. What possessions did the Israelites take with them?

3. Who guided the Israelites through the wilderness?

4. Which army chased after the Israelites?

5. When the Israelites reached the sea, where did they camp?

6. How did Moses command the sea to divide so the Israelites could cross to the other side?

7. Which sea did the Israelites cross through to escape the Egyptians?

8. How did God stop the Egyptians chasing the Israelites across the sea?

9. What happened to the Egyptian army?

10. What did the Israelites do when they reached the other side of the sea?

The ten COMMANDMENTS

Read Exodus 20:1-26. Answer the questions below.

1. To whom did God give the ten commandments?

2. What is the 5th commandment?

3. 'You shall not murder' is which commandment?

4. What were the ten commandments written on?

5. What is the 4th commandment?

6. Which commandment instructs us not to lie?

7. Which commandment forbids stealing?

8. Which commandment forbids making idols to worship God?

9. Where did Moses receive the commandments from God?

10. What is the 10th commandment?

The golden CALF

Read Exodus 32:1-35. Answer the questions below.

1. While Moses received the ten commandments, what did the Israelites do?

2. What metal was the calf made from?

3. How did the Israelites worship the calf?

4. How did God react to the golden calf?

5. What did Moses do when he saw the calf?

6. How did Moses destroy the golden calf?

7. Who claimed the golden calf simply came out of the fire?

8. How did Moses punish the Israelites for worshiping the golden calf?

9. How did God punish the Israelites for worshiping the golden calf?

10. At what place did the Israelites make the golden calf?

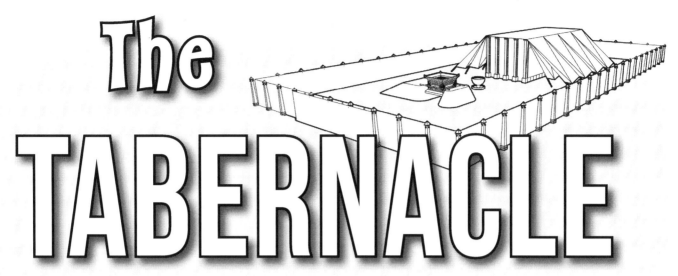

The TABERNACLE

Read Exodus 26:1-31:18. Answer the questions below.

1) Who was the first high priest?

2) What was the purpose of the tabernacle?

3) Where was the mercy seat located?

4) What was the mercy seat made out of?

5) Priests were chosen from which tribe of Israel?

6) Who did God put in charge of building the tabernacle?

7) In which book of the Torah are instructions for building the tabernacle found?

8) What type of oil was used to keep lamps burning in the tabernacle?

9) What was the purpose of the brazen altar?

10) The ark of the covenant was made from which type of wood?

Korah
REBELS

Read Numbers 16:1-50. Answer the questions below.

1) Korah was from which tribe of Israel?

2) Korah was the son of which man?

3) How many men did Korah gather to speak against the leaders of Israel?

4) Whose authority did Korah and the men challenge?

5) What did Moses do when he heard Korah's complaints?

6) What did Moses tell Korah and the men to do?

7) Whose tents did God say to move away from?

8) What did the earth do to Korah's men and their households?

9) What came into the camp and killed 14,700 people?

10) Who was the leader of the Israelites?

JOSHUA

Read Joshua 1:1-5:15, 10:1-43, and Judges 2:1-10. Answer the questions below.

1. Who did Joshua succeed as leader of Israel?

2. Where did Rahab hide the spies in Jericho?

3. What happened to the walls of Jericho after the Israelites blew their shofars?

4. The Israelites crossed which river to enter the Promised Land?

5. What did Joshua do after the Israelites crossed over the Jordan?

6. Among which people did Joshua divide the Promised Land?

7. How long did the sun stand still for Joshua?

8. Which nation deceived Joshua?

9. What type of weather helped Joshua defeat the Amorites?

10. How old was Joshua when he died?

Twelve spies
in CANAAN

Read Numbers 13:1-33. Answer the questions below.

1. How many tribes of Israel were camped in the wilderness?

2. At what place were the tribes camped?

3. How many spies did Moses send to Canaan?

4. Which route did Moses tell the spies to travel?

5. What did Moses ask the twelve spies to bring back from Canaan?

6. What type of people did the spies see in Canaan?

7. Which tribe of enemies did the spies find in Canaan?

8. How many days did the spies explore the land?

9. What fruit did the spies bring back from Canaan?

10. Which two spies wanted to go and conquer Canaan?

Balaam's DONKEY

Read Numbers 22–25, 31. Answer the questions below.

1. How many tribes of Israel were camped on the plains of Moab?

2. What was the name of the king of Moab?

3. Why did the king of Moab ask Balaam to come to Moab?

4. Who traveled with Balaam and his donkey?

5. In which book of the Bible is the story of Balaam and his donkey?

6. What animal spoke to Balaam?

7. What did Balaam do after the Angel of God spared his life?

8. How many times did Balaam bless the Israelites?

9. To defeat the Israelites, what did Balaam tell King Balak to do?

10. How many men from each tribe went into battle against the Midianites?

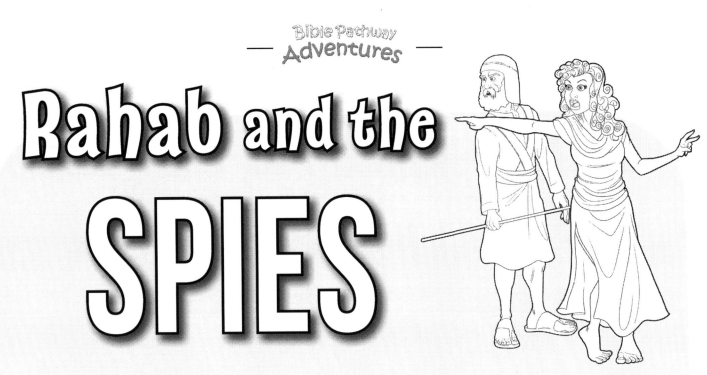

Rahab and the SPIES

Read Joshua 2:1-24. Answer the questions below.

1. Who sent two spies to the city of Jericho?

2. Where were the spies sent from?

3. Who were the two spies who went to spy out Jericho?

4. Where in Jericho was Rahab's house?

5. How did Rahab hide the spies?

6. Who sent a message to Rabab telling her to bring out the spies?

7. Where did the king's men look for the spies?

8. How did Rahab help the spies escape?

9. Why did Joshua spare the lives of Rahab and her family?

10. How did Rahab mark her house so she was spared by the Israelites?

GIDEON

Read Judges 6. Answer the questions below.

1. Why did God allow the Midianites to attack the Israelites?

2. Where was Gideon threshing wheat?

3. What message did the Angel give Gideon?

4. What food did Gideon prepare as a sacrifice?

5. What Midianite altar did Gideon destroy?

6. What object did Gideon place on the ground to receive a sign from God?

7. How many soldiers did Gideon have initially? From which tribes of Israel?

8. How many men lapped the water, putting their hands to their mouths?

9. What objects did Gideon and his army use to defeat the Midianites?

10. What insect does the Bible use to describe the number of Midianites in their camp?

RUTH & BOAZ

Read Ruth 1:1-4:17. Answer the questions below.

1. Where was Ruth born?

2. What was the name of Ruth's sister-in- law?

3. Who was Ruth's first husband?

4. With whom did Ruth move to Bethlehem?

5. Where did Ruth and Boaz first meet?

6. What did Boaz offer Ruth to eat?

7. On the threshing floor, where did Ruth sleep?

8. The next morning, what did Boaz give Ruth?

9. Boaz was of which tribe of Israel? (1 Chronicles 2)

10. What did Ruth and Boaz name their son?

SAMSON

Read Judges 13:1-16:31.
Answer the questions below.

1. Who told Samson's father that he would have a son?

2. What important instructions did an angel give Samson's mother?

3. What did Samson kill with his bare hands?

4. How did the wedding guests know the answer to Samson's riddle?

5. How many foxes did Samson catch?

6. How many Philistines did Samson kill with a donkey jawbone?

7. How many years did Samson judge the Israelites?

8. How much silver did each Philistine king offer Delilah to betray Samson?

9. When Samson's hair was cut off, what happened to him?

10. Which Philistine building did Samson destroy?

SAMSON & DELILAH

Read Judges 16:1-31. Answer the questions below.

1. The name of an Israelite set apart for God's service.

2. For how many years did Samson judge the Israelites?

3. How much silver was Delilah offered to betray Samson?

4. What was Delilah's nationality?

5. Where did Delilah live?

6. What did Delilah use to first bind Samson?

7. What did Delilah use to bind Samson a second time?

8. How many locks of Samson's hair did Delilah weave into her loom?

9. What did Samson finally tell Delilah was the secret of his strength?

10. When Samson was caught by the Philistines, how did they hold him?

SAMUEL

Read 1 Samuel 1:1-28, 8:1-10:27, and 28:1-25.
Answer the questions below.

1. When Samuel was called by God as a child, who did he think was calling?

2. What did Samuel's mother bring him each year?

3. Why did Samuel never cut his hair?

4. What did the Israelites demand from Samuel?

5. What did Samuel warn the Israelites a king would do?

6. Who did Samuel anoint as the first king of Israel?

7. Samuel was of which tribe of Israel?

8. What were the names of Samuel's two sons?

9. What did Samuel tell King Saul when he rose from the grave?

10. Where did Samuel go when he died? (1 Sam 28)

King
SAUL

Read 1 Samuel 8:1-10:27, 14:1-14, 28:1-25, and 31:1-13.
Answer the questions below.

1) Saul was of which tribe of Israel?

2) Which group of enemies did Saul fight many times?

3) Which Hebrew prophet anointed Saul as king?

4) What was the name of Saul's father?

5) Which son of Saul was good friends with David?

6) Who told Saul to fight the Amalekites?

7) Which son-in-law did Saul try to kill many times?

8) Whenever Saul was troubled by an evil spirit, what did David do?

9) Saul disobeyed God and visited which witch?

10) Saul died during which battle?

Witch of ENDOR

**Read Deuteronomy 18:9-14 and 1 Samuel 28-31.
Answer the questions below.**

① King Saul was king of which people?

② Which army wanted to fight the Israelites?

③ Why did King Saul want to talk to a witch?

④ In which town did King Saul talk to a witch?

⑤ Who did King Saul ask the witch to raise from the grave?

⑥ Why did King Saul want to talk to Samuel?

⑦ What did Samuel tell King Saul?

⑧ What happened to King Saul after he visited the witch of Endor?

⑨ Where in the Bible does God forbid trying to talk to dead people?

⑩ How did King Saul lose his life?

Ark is CAPTURED

Read 1 Samuel 4:1-6:21. Answer the questions below.

1. Which enemies did the Israelites fight?

2. In what place did the Israelites camp?

3. How many Israelites were killed by the Philistines?

4. Whose two sons died in battle?

5. What happened to Eli when he heard about the ark?

6. What statue did the Philistines place the ark beside?

7. What happened to the statue of Dagon?

8. What did God send on the people of Ashdod?

9. For how many months did the Philistines keep the ark?

10. How did the Philistines return the ark to the Israelites?

DAVID & GOLIATH

Read 1 Samuel 15:1-18:7. Answer the questions below.

1. What was David's job when he was young?

2. Which prophet anointed David as king?

3. What musical instrument did David play for King Saul?

4. In which place did the Israelite and Philistine armies set up camp?

5. How tall was Goliath?

6. How many days did Goliath challenge Israel to send a man to fight him?

7. Who gave David permission to fight Goliath?

8. How many stones did David pick out of the stream?

9. How did David kill Goliath?

10. How did the people of Israel celebrate David's great victory?

Kings of the BIBLE

Read Numbers 22, 1 Samuel 9-16, Daniel 1-6, 2 Chronicles 3, Esther 1-3, and Matthew 14. Answer the questions below.

1. Who was the first king of Israel?

2. Which prophet anointed David as king?

3. Which king had Daniel thrown to the lions?

4. Which king wanted Balaam to curse the Israelites?

5. Which king built the first temple in Jerusalem?

6. What was David's job before he became king?

7. Which king saw the writing on the wall?

8. Which king's wives included Vashti and Esther?

9. Which king had a dream about a statue made of different metals?

10. Which king imprisoned John the Baptist?

People of the

TORAH

Read Genesis 5-6, 11-12, 25, 32, 37, Exodus 2, 4, Numbers 22, and Deuteronomy 31. Answer the questions below.

1. Who was the false prophet who tried to curse Israel?

2. Who was the mother of Jacob and Esau?

3. How old was Noah when he entered the Ark?

4. Who was sold into slavery in Egypt by his brothers?

5. Who was Zipporah's husband?

6. What was the name of Noah's father?

7. Who became leader of the Israelites after the death of Moses?

8. Who was Moses' brother?

9. Who left the house of his father Terah and traveled to Canaan?

10. Whose name was changed to Israel?

King SOLOMON

Read 1 Kings 1-11; 1 Chronicles 28-29, and 2 Chronicles 1-9. Answer the questions below.

1. Who was Solomon's father?

2. Which priest anointed Solomon?

3. Where was Solomon anointed?

4. Solomon asked God for which gift?

5. How many years did it take Solomon to build the temple?

6. Which king helped Solomon build the temple and a palace?

7. What gifts did the Queen of Sheba give Solomon?

8. How many wives did Solomon have?

9. For how long did Solomon rule Israel?

10. Which son of Solomon succeeded him as king of Israel?

Queen of
SHEBA

Read 1 Kings 1:11 and 10:1-13. Answer the questions below.

① Why did the queen visit Solomon?

② What gifts did the queen bring with her?

③ How did the queen describe Solomon's servants?

④ What impressed the queen about Solomon?

⑤ What did the queen say about God?

⑥ In which city was the temple?

⑦ Who was Solomon's mother?

⑧ What did Solomon do with the wood that Hiram brought him?

⑨ What gifts did Solomon give the queen?

⑩ After the queen and her servants left Jerusalem, where did they go?

Hezekiah's
GOLD

Read 2 Kings 18:1-19:37. Answer the questions below.

1) How old was Hezekiah when he began to reign Judah?

2) What was the name of Hezekiah's father?

3) Which king attacked Judah?

4) Which prophet did Hezekiah ask for help?

5) Which city did the king of Assyria order his soldiers to attack?

6) How much money did the King of Assyria demand?

7) What did Hezekiah give the Assyrians?

8) What building did Hezekiah take this metal from?

9) Which spiritual being killed 185,000 Assyrian soldiers?

10) Whose commandments did the king of Judah keep?

ISAIAH

Read 2 Kings 20:1-2, Isaiah 1:1-31, 7:1-8:4, and 38:1-22. Answer the questions below.

1. What was Isaiah's job?

2. Who was Isaiah's father?

3. What did Isaiah say that God likened sin to?

4. What did Isaiah tell King Hezekiah while he was sick?

5. How many children did Isaiah have?

6. To whom did Isaiah prophesy?

7. How many kings of Judah reigned while Isaiah was a prophet?

8. Isaiah was from which tribe of Israel?

9. What did Isaiah tell Hezekiah would happen because he had showed the King of Babylon his treasures?

10. How many chapters are in the Book of Isaiah?

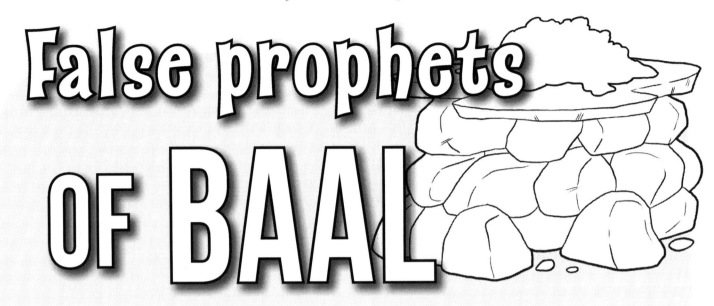

False prophets OF BAAL

Read 1 Kings 18. Answer the questions below.

1. For how many years had there been no rain?

2. How many false prophets did Elijah summon?

3. On what mountain did Elijah meet the false prophets?

4. What did the false prophets do to get Baal's attention?

5. What test did Elijah set the false prophets?

6. What animal did Elijah sacrifice on the altar?

7. What did the fire of God burn up?

8. Why did Elijah choose twelve stones to build an altar?

9. How many jars were used to pour water on the sacrifice and wood?

10. What did the people do when they saw the fire of God?

Josiah and the
TORAH

Read 2 Kings 22-23. Answer the questions below.

1. How old was Josiah when he became king?

2. Who was Josiah's father? (2 Kings 21)

3. What materials were purchased to repair the temple in Jerusalem?

4. Who found the Scroll of the Torah?

5. Who read the Scroll of the Torah to Josiah?

6. What did Josiah do when he heard the Torah?

7. What did King Josiah have destroyed?

8. Which meal did Josiah tell the Israelites to observe?

9. What happened after Josiah read the Torah to the people?

10. Where did Josiah burn the Asherah pole from the temple?

King NEBUCHADNEZZAR

Read Daniel 1:1-4:37. Answer the questions below.

1. Nebuchadnezzar ruled which kingdom?

2. What name did the king give Daniel?

3. Which king of Judah did Nebuchadnezzar take back to Babylon?

4. When Daniel interpreted the king's dreams, how was he rewarded?

5. In Nebuchadnezzar's dream what did the different metals of the statue represent?

6. How tall was the golden statue that the king had made?

7. Where did the king have the golden image placed?

8. Who refused to worship the king's golden image?

9. How did the king punish the boys for not worshipping the statue?

10. Who was the fourth person in the furnace with Daniel's friends?

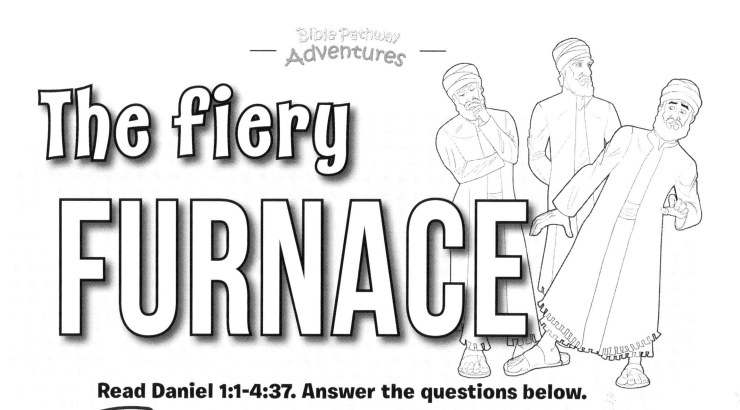

The fiery FURNACE

Read Daniel 1:1-4:37. Answer the questions below.

1. Daniel and his friends were taken prisoner back to which kingdom?

2. What were the names of Daniel's three friends?

3. Which king had set up the golden statue?

4. How did the three Hebrew men disobey the king of Babylon?

5. How did the king punish the men?

6. How many times hotter than normal was the furnace?

7. What happened to the men who threw the Hebrews into the fire?

8. What did the king see when he looked in the furnace?

9. What happened to the three men after they came out of the fire?

10. When the men came out of fire, what did the officials see?

Daniel and the
LIONS

Read Daniel 1:1-2:49 and 5:1-6:28. Answer the questions below.

1. What was Daniel's new name in Babylon?

2. What did Daniel do for King Nebuchadnezzar?

3. What did Daniel eat instead of the king's meat and drink?

4. Who plotted to kill Daniel?

5. What happened to Daniel after he gave thanks to God by his open window?

6. Why was Daniel thrown to the lions?

7. Which king had Daniel thrown to the lions?

8. How was the lion's den sealed?

9. How was Daniel protected from the lions in the den?

10. What was done to the Magi who had accused Daniel?

Jonah and the BIG FISH

Read Jonah 1-4. Answer the questions below.

1. To which city did God ask Jonah to take His message of repentance?

2. Where did Jonah try to run to instead of going to Nineveh?

3. In which city did Jonah board a ship?

4. Who threw Jonah overboard?

5. What happened after Jonah was thrown overboard?

6. How long was Jonah inside the fish?

7. What did Jonah tell the people when he reached Nineveh?

8. What did the people do to show they believed God's message?

9. What did Jonah do after God decided not to destroy the city?

10. What happened to the plant that grew up over Jonah's head?

NEHEMIAH

**Read Nehemiah 1:1-4:23 and 6:1-8:18.
Answer the questions below.**

1. In what kingdom was Nehemiah living?

2. What was Nehemiah's job?

3. How did Nehemiah hear about news about Jerusalem?

4. What did Nehemiah ask the king of Persia?

5. What did Sanballat, Tobia and Gesham accuse Nehemiah of doing?

6. Who was the high priest?

7. Which men repaired the section of the wall over the Horse Gate?

8. How long did it take to rebuild the walls of Jerusalem?

9. What happened when the Israelites' enemies heard the walls were rebuilt?

10. In chapter 8, what Appointed Time (Feast) did the people celebrate?

Esther saves HER PEOPLE

Read Esther 1:1-9:32. Answer the questions below.

1. Who was the king of Persia?

2. Which family member did Mordecai help raise?

3. Who disobeyed the king by not coming when he commanded?

4. Why did Haman have a set of gallows made?

5. When Mordecai left Esther at the palace, what instructions did he give her?

6. What did Esther ask Mordecai and the Hebrews to do before she saw the king?

7. What did the king do when Esther came before him uninvited?

8. Who did Queen Esther invite to her banquets?

9. Who wanted to destroy all the Hebrews in the kingdom?

10. How did the king stop the destruction of the Hebrews?

The story OF JOB

Read Job 1:1-2:13 and 41:1-42:1-17. Answer the questions below.

1. In which land did Job and his family live?

2. Before his trials, how many children did Job have?

3. How did Job's children die?

4. What did God say to Satan (the adversary) about Job?

5. Who encouraged Job to curse God?

6. When Job's friends arrived, how long did they sit in silence?

7. What did Job's friends give him?

8. From where did God answer Job?

9. Where did the Leviathan live?

10. After Job repented, what did God do for him?

Twelve tribes OF ISRAEL

Read Numbers 2:1-34, 13, 18:7, Judges 6, Philippians 3:5, Romans 1:1, and James 1:2. Answer the questions below.

① To which tribe did Joshua belong?

② How many cities were the Levites given?

③ To which tribe did Paul belong?

④ To which tribe did Gideon belong?

⑤ Which tribe received no inheritance of land?

⑥ Which tribe served as priests?

⑦ Which three tribes camped on the north side of the tabernacle?

⑧ Which two tribes of Israel were not named after sons of Jacob?

⑨ Which tribes settled on the east side of the Jordan River?

⑩ In James 1:2, to whom did James address his letter?

Women of the BIBLE

Read Genesis 27, Numbers 26, Judges 5, 2 Samuel 11, Ruth, Esther 2, Luke 1, Matthew 1, and Acts 16. Answer the questions below.

1. What relationship was Ruth to Naomi?

2. Who was Jacob's mother?

3. What was the name of Moses' sister?

4. Which woman was a seller of purple goods?

5. With whom did David commit adultery?

6. What was the name of Ahasuerus' new queen?

7. What was the name of Yeshua's mother?

8. What did Ruth do to Boaz while he was sleeping?

9. Which female judge described herself as 'a mother in Israel'?

10. What was the name of John the Baptist's mother?

Mothers of the BIBLE

Read Genesis 2, 16, 21, 25, 27, 35, Exodus 2, Judges 5, 1 Kings 1, and Luke 2. Answer the questions below.

1 Who was Jacob's mother?

2 Who was the mother of Isaac?

3 Who was the mother of Joseph and Benjamin?

4 Which mother in the Bible had a set of twins?

5 Who was the first mother mentioned in the Bible?

6 What was the name of Yeshua's mother?

7 Which female judge said she was "a mother in Israel"?

8 Who was the mother of King Solomon?

9 Whose mother placed him in a basket by the river?

10 Who was the Egyptian slave who gave birth to Ishmael?

Fathers of the

BIBLE

**Read Genesis 11, 22, 31, Exodus 20, Matthew 1,
Luke 1, 8, 15, and Acts 16. Answer the questions below.**

1. Who was the father of Abraham?

2. Whose father was so pleased to see him that he killed a fatted calf?

3. Which father asked Yeshua to help his daughter who was dying?

4. Who stole her father's household gods?

5. What nationality was Timothy's father?

6. Who was the father of John the Baptist?

7. Who was the father of Solomon?

8. Whose father was prepared to sacrifice him on an altar?

9. Which commandment says to honor your father and mother?

10. Who was the father of King David?

John the BAPTIST

Read Matthew 3, 11, 14, 17, Mark 1, Luke 1 and 7, and John 1, 3, 10. Answer the questions below.

1. What was the name of John's mother?

2. What was the name of John's father?

3. In which river did John baptize the people?

4. In which wilderness did John live?

5. About which man did John say he was unworthy to untie His sandals?

6. From which region did Yeshua come to be baptized by John?

7. John's clothes were made of what type of animal hair?

8. What type of insect did John like to eat?

9. What did John say when he saw Yeshua near the Jordan River?

10. Which ruler ordered John's arrest?

An angel visits
MARY

Read Luke 1. Answer the questions below.

① To which city did God send His angel to visit Mary?

② In which month of Elizabeth's pregnancy did the angel visit Mary?

③ What was the name of the angel who visited Mary?

④ To which man was Mary engaged (betrothed)?

⑤ What did the angel first say to Mary when he saw her?

⑥ How did Mary react when she saw the angel?

⑦ What message did the angel give Mary?

⑧ What name did the angel tell Mary to give the child?

⑨ Why was Mary surprised at what the angel told her?

⑩ How did the angel tell Mary she would have a child?

Birth of the MESSIAH

Read Matthew 1-2, Mark 1, Luke 2, and Micah 5:2. Answer the questions below.

1. What name did the angel Gabriel tell Mary to name her child?

2. Who ordered a census of the entire Roman world at the time of Yeshua's birth?

3. Why did Mary and Joseph travel to Bethlehem for the census?

4. In which town was Yeshua born?

5. Who was king of Judea at this time?

6. Yeshua was of which tribe of Israel?

7. What did the Old Testament prophet Micah say about Yeshua's birth?

8. How many magi (Wise Men) visited Yeshua after He was born?

9. What did King Herod do after the Magi tricked him?

10. To which land did Joseph, Mary, and Yeshua flee until Herod had died?

The shepherd's VISIT

Read Luke 2. Answer the questions below.

1. Why were the shepherds out in the fields at night?

2. What type of angel appeared to the shepherds?

3. How did the shepherds react when they saw the angel?

4. What message did the angel give the shepherds?

5. What did the angel say the shepherds would find when they visited the Messiah?

6. To which town did the shepherds go to visit the Messiah?

7. What did the shepherds see when they arrived in the town?

8. What did the shepherds tell Mary and Joseph?

9. What was the name of the Messiah?

10. After seeing the child, what did the shepherds do next?

The MAGI

Read Matthew 1:1-2:23. Answer the questions below.

① Who was king of Judea at the time of Yeshua's birth?

② How did the Magi (Wise Men) know that Yeshua had been born?

③ Who did the Magi ask to see when they arrived in Jerusalem?

④ To which town did Herod send the Magi?

⑤ What did the Magi do when they saw Yeshua?

⑥ How many Magi does the Bible say came to visit young Yeshua?

⑦ What gifts did the Magi give Yeshua?

⑧ Why did the Magi not return to Herod?

⑨ Where else in the Bible are the Magi mentioned?

⑩ What did Herod do after he was tricked by the Magi?

Presentation in the
TEMPLE

Read Luke 2:1-38. Answer the questions below.

1. Who told Mary to name her son Yeshua?

2. In which city was the temple?

3. On which day was Yeshua circumcized?

4. Why did Mary and Joseph present Yeshua in the temple?

5. Who said, "for my eyes have seen your salvation…" when he saw Yeshua?

6. What did Anna do at the temple every day?

7. How old was Anna when she saw Yeshua?

8. Anna was of which tribe of Israel?

9. What offering did Mary and Joseph make in the temple?

10. Where did Mary and Joseph take Yeshua after they presented Him at the temple?

The twelve DISCIPLES

Read Matthew 8, 17, 19-21, Luke 5, Mark 2-3, John 1, 13, 18, 21, and Acts 1:12-26. Answer the questions below.

1. Which disciple was a tax collector?

2. Who were the first two disciples to be called?

3. Which disciple tried to walk on water, like Yeshua?

4. Which three disciples were from Bethsaida?

5. What event did Peter, James and John witness on a mountain with Yeshua?

6. What did Yeshua send two disciples to fetch on His entry into Jerusalem?

7. Which disciple betrayed Yeshua?

8. What did Yeshua do for each disciple during the Last Supper?

9. After Yeshua's death, which disciple looked after His mother Mary?

10. What was the name of the disciple who replaced Judas?

The TEMPLE

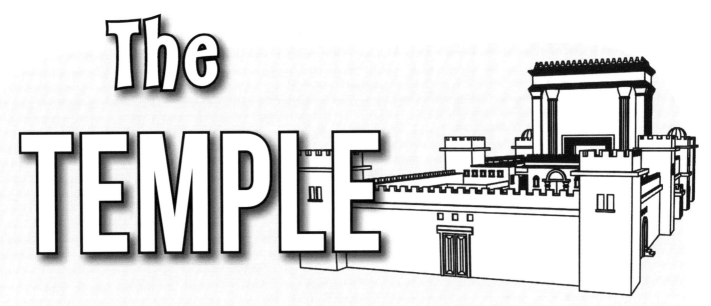

Read Leviticus 16, Ezra 1, 1 Chronicles 28, 1 Kings 6, John 2-3, Matthew 21 and Acts 3. Answer the questions below.

1. Which king built the first temple in Jerusalem?

2. Why didn't God allow King David to build a temple?

3. Where did Cyrus the Great tell the Israelites to rebuild the temple?

4. Where in the first temple was the ark of the covenant kept?

5. On which day of the year could the high priest enter the Holy of Holies?

6. In which part of the temple did Yeshua teach?

7. How many times did Yeshua cleanse the temple?

8. How long did Herod the Great take to build another temple?

9. On which three Appointed Times (Feasts) were men commanded to travel to Jerusalem?

10. In Acts 3:12, who was Peter speaking to?

Wedding feast AT CANA

Read John 2:1-12. Answer the questions below.

1. To what celebration was Yeshua invited?

2. In which town was the celebration held?

3. What was the name of Yeshua's mother?

4. Apart from Yeshua, who else was invited to the wedding?

5. How many stone water jars were at the wedding?

6. How many gallons of fluid could each jar hold?

7. With what liquid did Yeshua tell the servants to fill the jars?

8. What did Yeshua turn water into?

9. After the Master of the feast tasted the wine, who did he call for?

10. After the wedding feast, to which town did Yeshua go next?

CAPERNAUM

**Read Matthew 11, 17, Luke 4-5, 7, and Mark 1-2.
Answer the questions below.**

1. What type of village was Capernaum?

2. Which disciple had a house in Capernaum?

3. Which four disciples lived in Capernaum?

4. Capernaum was located on the shore of which sea?

5. Yeshua healed the servant of which official?

6. Where did Peter find the money to pay the temple tax?

7. How did the paralytic man enter the house in Capernaum where Yeshua was staying?

8. On which day of the week did Yeshua teach at the synagogue?

9. Whose mother-in- law did Yeshua heal?

10. What was wrong with the man who interrupted Yeshua teaching at the synagogue?

Tempted in the WILDERNESS

**Read Deuteronomy 6-8, Matthew 4, Mark 1, and Luke 4.
Answer the questions below.**

1. Who led Yeshua into the wilderness to be tempted?

2. Whose job was it to tempt Yeshua?

3. For how many days and nights did Yeshua fast and pray?

4. When did the Tempter come to tempt Yeshua?

5. How many times was Yeshua tempted?

6. What was Yeshua tempted to turn into loaves of bread?

7. Where did the Tempter tell Yeshua to jump from?

8. What did the Tempter promise if Yeshua would bow down and worship him?

9. Which book of the Bible did Yeshua use to answer the Tempter?

10. After the third temptation, what happened?

Bible Pathway Adventures

Sermon on the
MOUNT

Read Matthew 5-7 and Luke 6, 11. Answer the questions below.

1. Who was Yeshua speaking to?

2. Why did Yeshua say to be glad when people persecute you because of your faith in Him?

3. Who did Yeshua say would inherit the earth?

4. What happens to treasure on earth?

5. What should you do when someone asks you to do something extra?

6. How are we meant to treat others?

7. What did Yeshua tell people to seek first?

8. What did Yeshua tell people not to worry about?

9. Where did Yeshua tell people to pray?

10. What will not pass away until heaven and earth pass away?

Feeding the 5000

Read Matthew 14, Mark 6, Luke 9, and John 6.
Answer the questions below.

1. What food did a young boy have with him?

2. How many people had gathered to hear Yeshua teach?

3. What is another name for the Sea of Galilee?

4. In which place were Yeshua and His disciples when He fed the people?

5. Why did Yeshua ask Philip, "Where shall we buy bread for the people to eat?

6. What did Yeshua do when He held the loaves of bread?

7. After the people had eaten, how many baskets of food were filled with leftovers?

8. In what region did this event take place?

9. Which Appointed Time (Feast) was about to begin?

10. Where did Yeshua go after he had fed the crowd?

Jairus' DAUGHTER

Read Matthew 9:18-26 and Mark 5:21-43.
Answer the questions below.

1. Whose daughter had fallen asleep?

2. Yeshua told the man, "Don't be afraid, just _____."

3. Which three disciples went with Yeshua to the house?

4. When Yeshua and His disciples arrived at Jairus' house, what was everyone doing?

5. How old was Jairus' daughter?

6. Why did the people at Jairus' house laugh at Yeshua?

7. What did Yeshua say to Jairus' daughter while she was sleeping?

8. What happened after Jairus daughter woke up?

9. In what region did this miracle take place?

10. What instructions did Yeshua give Jairus and his family?

Zacchaeus the TAX COLLECTOR

Read Luke 19:1-10. Answer the questions below.

1. What was Zacchaeus' job?

2. Was Zacchaeus rich or poor?

3. In which city did this story take place?

4. Where did Yeshua want to stay that day?

5. Why did Zacchaeus climb a tree?

6. What type of tree did Zacchaeus climb?

7. Yeshua was of which tribe of Israel?

8. Who did Yeshua say He came to save? (Luke 19:10)

9. How much of his goods did Zacchaeus promise the poor?

10. How many times did Zacchaeus promise to pay back the people he had defrauded?

Parable of the TALENTS

Read Matthew 25:14-30. Answer the questions below.

1) How many talents did the Master give his first servant?

2) How many talents did the Master give his second servant?

3) How many talents did the third servant receive?

4) What did the first servant do with his talents?

5) What did the second servant do with his talents?

6) What did the third servant do with his talent?

7) What did the Master say to his first and second servants when he came to see them?

8) What excuse did the third servant give his Master for doing nothing with his talent?

9) How did the Master react to the third servant's excuse?

10) What did the Master do with that servant's talent?

Parable of the wise & foolish VIRGINS

Read Matthew 25:1-13. Answer the questions below.

1) How many virgins went to meet the bridegroom?

2) How many virgins were wise?

3) What happened when the bridegroom was delayed?

4) At what time did the virgins hear the bridegroom was on His way to meet them?

5) What were the virgins told to do?

6) What did the wise virgins take with them to meet the bridegroom?

7) What did the foolish virgins take with them to meet the bridegroom?

8) What did the foolish virgins ask the wise virgins?

9) What happened while the foolish virgins went to buy oil?

10) Why did the bridegroom not let the foolish virgins into the wedding?

Parable of the good SAMARITAN

Read Luke 10:25-37. Answer the questions below.

1. Where was the traveler going in the story?

2. What happened to the traveler on this road?

3. Who was the first man to walk past?

4. Who was the second man to walk past?

5. Who was the third man to see the traveler?

6. What did the Samaritan do to help the traveler?

7. How much did he pay the innkeeper?

8. Who stood up and asked Yeshua how to inherit eternal life?

9. How did Yeshua answer this man?

10. When Yeshua asked the Torah teacher who was the neighbor, how did he answer?

Parable of the PRODIGAL SON

Read Luke 15:11-32. Answer the questions below.

1. How many sons did the father have?

2. Which son asked his father for his inheritance?

3. After he left home, where did the son go?

4. What happened in the country where the son went?

5. After the son wasted his money, what job did he get?

6. Why did the son decide to return home?

7. Who was not happy about the son's return?

8. What did the father do when he saw his youngest son in the distance?

9. What did the father give his son when he arrived home?

10. What did the father do to celebrate his youngest son's return?

Woman at the WELL

Read John 4:1-45. Answer the questions below.

1. Why did Yeshua leave Judea?

2. After Yeshua left Judea, what place did he set out for?

3. What was the name of the well where Yeshua talked with the woman?

4. From what region was the woman who came to draw water?

5. Where did Yeshua's disciples go while He spoke to the woman?

6. How many husbands had the woman had?

7. True worshipers will worship the Father in _____ and truth.

8. Who did Yeshua tell the woman was the Messiah?

9. Whoever _____ of the water I will give him will never be thirsty again.

10. Why did many townspeople start to believe Yeshua was the Messiah?

The TRANSFIGURATION

Read Matthew 16-17, Mark 9, and Luke 9.
Answer the questions below.

1. Which three disciples did Yeshua take with him to a high mountain?

2. How did the disciples feel?

3. What happened to Yeshua's clothes while He was praying?

4. Which two Old Testament prophets appeared?

5. What did Peter offer to do for Yeshua and the prophets?

6. What did the prophets talk about?

7. What appeared and covered the men?

8. What did the voice in the cloud say to the men?

9. Who did the voice belong to?

10. When did Yeshua and His disciples come down from the mountain?

Bible Pathway Adventures

Triumphal ENTRY

Read Matthew 21, Mark 11, Luke 19, and John 12.
Answer the questions below.

1. Which Appointed Time (Feast) were Yeshua and His disciples traveling to Jerusalem to keep?

2. What part of Judea was Yeshua from?

3. In which village did the disciples find a donkey and colt?

4. How many disciples fetched the two animals?

5. Who entered Jerusalem on a young donkey?

6. How did the crowd greet Yeshua?

7. As Yeshua rode by, what did the crowd say to Him?

8. After Yeshua entered Jerusalem, which place of worship did he go to?

9. What meal takes place at the start of the Feast of Unleavened Bread?

10. Which prophet's words were fulfilled that day?

Yeshua clears
THE TEMPLE

Read Matthew 21:12-17. Answer the questions below.

1. Who went with Yeshua to the temple?

2. When Yeshua arrived at the temple, what were some people doing?

3. Yeshua made a whip out of what material?

4. In which city was the temple located?

5. What did Yeshua accuse the traders of doing?

6. What animals were being sold in the temple?

7. What did Yeshua do to the moneychangers?

8. Which Judean ruler built this temple?

9. What did Yeshua tell the traders that His House (temple) was?

10. What Appointed Time (Feast) was about to start?

JUDAS

Read Luke 6, Mark 14:1-11, John 12:1-13:30,
Luke 22, Matthew 10:1-6, 26:1-27:10, and Acts 1.
Answer the questions below.

1. Judas was one of the twelve _____?

2. What did Yeshua give Judas as a sign that he was to betray Him?

3. Who paid Judas to betray Yeshua?

4. How much money was Judas given to betray Yeshua?

5. Where did Judas betray Yeshua?

6. How did Judas betray Yeshua?

7. In the garden, how did Judas address Yeshua?

8. What was the name of the field purchased with the money Judas returned?

9. After Yeshua rose to heaven, who were the two men put forward to replace Judas?

10. Which man was finally chosen to replace Judas?

The last SUPPER

**Read Matthew 26, Mark 14, Luke 22, and John 13.
Answer the questions below.**

(1) In which city did Yeshua and His disciples eat the meal?

(2) Which of God's Appointed Times (Feasts) was about to begin?

(3) How many disciples were at the Last Supper?

(4) Which disciple did not want Yeshua to wash his feet?

(5) What did Yeshua and His disciples eat and drink at the meal?

(6) What did Yeshua say to His disciples when He broke the bread?

(7) What new commandment did Yeshua give His disciples?

(8) During the meal, what did the disciples argue about?

(9) Which disciple left the room to betray Yeshua?

(10) After the men finished the meal, where did they go?

GETHSEMANE

**Read Matthew 26, Mark 14, Luke 22, and John 18.
Answer the questions below.**

(1) Which garden did Yeshua go to pray in before He was arrested
by the religious leaders?

(2) While Yeshua was praying, what happened to Peter, James, and John?

(3) What did Yeshua say to the disciples when He found them sleeping?

(4) Which disciple did Yeshua warn would deny Him three times?

(5) How did Judas betray Yeshua?

(6) Who appeared to Yeshua in the garden to give Him strength?

(7) Which people did the religious leaders send to arrest Yeshua?

(8) Who cut off the ear of the high priest's servant?

(9) What happened to the disciples after Yeshua was arrested?

(10) After the Temple guards arrested Yeshua, where did they take Him?

Armor of GOD

Read Ephesians 6:10-20. Answer the questions below.

1. Have your feet fitted with the gospel of _____.

2. Put on the breastplate of _____.

3. Stand therefore, having the belt of _____ buckled around your waist.

4. We do not wrestle against _____ and blood.

5. Put on the whole _____ of God.

6. Shoes for your _____.

7. Take the _____ of salvation.

8. Keep alert with all _____.

9. Finally, be _____ in God, and in the strength of His might.

10. The _____ of the Spirit, which is the word of God.

Yeshua before PILATE

**Read Matthew 27, Mark 15, Luke 23, and John 18-19.
Answer the questions below.**

1. Why did the Sanhedrin need Pilate to approve Yeshua's death?

2. Who took Yeshua to see Pilate?

3. Where did Yeshua stand before Pilate?

4. What did the religious leaders accuse Yeshua before Pilate of doing?

5. How did Yeshua answer most of Pilate's questions?

6. Which king ruled Galilee and was in Jerusalem at that time?

7. What did the crowd demand Pilate do to Yeshua?

8. Which prisoner did Pilate release?

9. Who sent a warning to Pilate not to hurt Yeshua?

10. Why did Pilate wash his hands before the people?

Death on the STAKE

Read Matthew 27:32-56. Answer the questions below.

1. Who sentenced Yeshua to die?

2. Who was forced to carry Yeshua's crossbeam through the streets of Jerusalem?

3. At what place was Yeshua nailed to the stake?

4. What was written on the sign above Yeshua's head?

5. What did Yeshua cry out while He was nailed to the stake?

6. Who was crucified next to Yeshua?

7. After Yeshua died, how long did darkness cover the land?

8. Who asked Pilate for Yeshua's body?

9. What did the Roman soldier use to pierce Yeshua's side?

10. What was Yeshua wrapped in before He was buried?

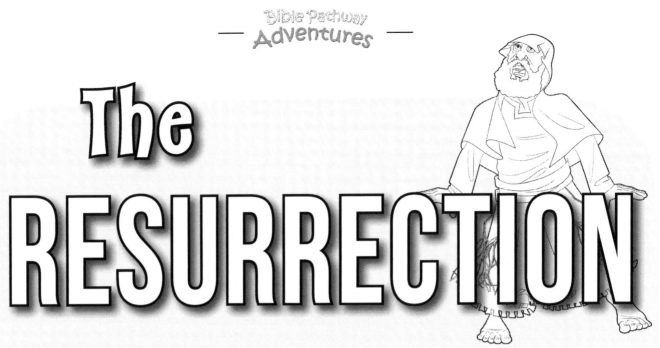

The RESURRECTION

Read Matthew 28, Mark 16, Luke 24, John 20, and Acts 1.
Answer the questions below.

1. Who rolled away Yeshua's tomb stone?

2. During which Appointed Time was Yeshua raised from the grave?

3. What did the priests give the Roman guards to keep quiet?

4. Who met Yeshua outside the tomb?

5. When Mary Magdalene, Mary mother of James, and Salome went to the tomb with their spices, what did they find?

6. What did the two strangers say to the women outside the tomb?

7. Which disciple doubted Yeshua was alive?

8. The disciples went fishing on which Sea?

9. How long did Yeshua stay on earth after His resurrection before He rose to Heaven?

10. What were Yeshua's final instructions to His disciples?

Road to EMMAUS

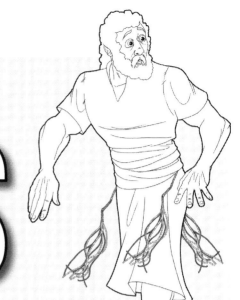

Read Luke 24:13-35. Answer the questions below.

1. Yeshua's death and resurrection took place during which Appointed Time?

2. How many disciples headed to Emmaus?

3. How many miles was the journey from Jerusalem to Emmaus?

4. Who met the two disciples on the road to Emmaus?

5. How did the disciples describe Yeshua to the stranger?

6. What did the disciples tell the stranger the women at the tomb had seen?

7. What scriptures did the stranger use to prove He was the Messiah?

8. When the disciples reached Emmaus, what did they do?

9. When did the disciples recognize Yeshua?

10. What happened as soon as the disciples recognized Yeshua?

The ASCENSION

Read Matthew 28:16-20, Mark 16:19-20, John 21 and Acts 1:1-12. Answer the questions below.

1. After Yeshua rose from the grave, how long did He stay on earth before He rose to Heaven?

2. After Yeshua appeared to His disciples in Jerusalem, where did they next meet Him?

3. Who dove into the water and swam towards Yeshua?

4. What did Yeshua ask Peter three times?

5. What did Yeshua promise His disciples before He rose to Heaven?

6. Where did Yeshua say His disciples would go and tell people about Him?

7. On which mount did Yeshua ascend to Heaven?

8. As Yeshua ascended, what hid Him from the eyes of those watching?

9. Who appeared to the disciples after Yeshua rose to Heaven?

10. What did these men tell the disciples?

Feast of PENTECOST

Read Exodus 19-20, Leviticus 23, Deuteronomy 16, and Acts 2-3. Answer the questions below.

1. From which mountain did God give His commandments?

2. How many days did Moses remain on the mountain to receive the commandments?

3. How many tribes camped at the foot of the mountain?

4. Which of the commandments is: Remember the Sabbath?

5. What is the fifth commandment?

6. In Acts 2, what sound did the disciples hear when they arrived at the temple?

7. What did the people hear when the disciples began speaking to them?

8. Which disciple stood up and spoke to the people about Yeshua?

9. In Acts 2:41, how many people repented and were baptized that day?

10. In which city did the disciples celebrate Shavuot?

Feast of
TABERNACLES

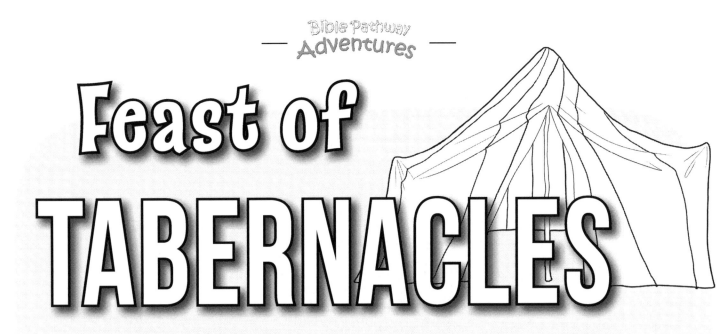

Read Leviticus 23, Numbers 29, Deuteronomy 16, Zechariah 14, and 1 Kings 8:2-21. Answer the questions below.

1. How long did God tell people to keep the Appointed Time of Sukkot?

2. How many days is Sukkot?

3. On which Appointed Time are people told to live in booths (sukkahs)?

4. When does Sukkot start?

5. What did God tell people to do during Sukkot?

6. At what time of the year does Sukkot take place?

7. On what days during Sukkot are people instructed to hold a sacred assembly?

8. Which historical event in the book of Exodus does Sukkot remind us?

9. Which king dedicated the temple during Sukkot?

10. What will be the punishment for nations not keeping Sukkot during the Millennial Reign? (Zechariah 14)

Philip and the ETHIOPIAN

Read Acts 8:26-40. Answer the questions below.

1. What did the Angel of God say to Philip?

2. Who did Philip meet on the road?

3. Why had the Ethiopian visited Jerusalem?

4. What was the Ethiopian's job?

5. What type of transport was the Ethiopian using?

6. What did the Holy Spirit tell Philip?

7. What scriptures was the Ethiopian reading?

8. Who did Philip explain the scriptures were speaking about?

9. When they came to some water, what did the Ethiopian want to do?

10. After the Ethiopian was baptized, what happened to Philip?

Road to DAMASCUS

Read Acts 9:1-25. Answer the questions below.

1. What was the name of Saul's hometown?

2. Who approved of the stoning of Stephen?

3. Why did Saul travel to Damascus?

4. Who gave Saul letters to the synagogues in Damascus?

5. What did Saul see on the road to Damascus?

6. Who spoke to Saul on the road to Damascus?

7. For how many days was Saul blinded?

8. Who was the disciple that God used to restore Saul's eyesight?

9. What did Saul teach in the synagogues while he stayed in Damascus?

10. How did Saul escape from Damascus?

Paul's LETTERS

Read Ephesians 6, Romans 12, 1 Corinthians 3, 11, 13, 16, Romans 2, 7, Galatians 5, 1 Timothy 6, and 1 Thessalonians 5. Answer the questions below.

1. Children, _____ your parents. (Ephesians 6:1)

2. Bless those who _____ you. (Romans 12:14)

3. Let all you do be done in _____. (1 Corinthians 16:14)

4. Do not be conformed to this world but be _____ by the renewing of your minds. (Romans 12:2)

5. You are God's temple and God's _____ dwells in you. (1 Cor 3:16)

6. Give _____ in all circumstances... (1 Thessalonians. 5:16)

7. The Torah is summed up in a single _____: You shall love your _____ as yourself. (Galatians 5:14)

8. We brought _____ into the world and take nothing out of it. (1 Timothy 6:7)

9. The _____ is holy, and the commandment is holy... (Romans 7:12)

10. Be _____ of me, just as I also am of Christ. (1 Corinthians 11:1)

Paul before KING AGRIPPA

Read Acts 25:1-26:32 and Philippians 3:5.
Answer the questions below.

(1) In which city was Paul kept prisoner?

(2) Who did Paul say he met on the road to Damascus?

(3) Which ruler accused Paul of being crazy?

(4) What was the name of King Agrippa's wife?

(5) Who gave Paul permission to persecute followers of Yeshua?

(6) Paul was what type of religious leader?

(7) Who was Paul given permission to meet and plead his case?

(8) Who was the Roman governor of Judea?

(9) When Paul stood in front of King Agrippa, what was he bound with?

(10) Why did Paul say the Judeans tried to kill him?

PRISCILLA & AQUILA

Read Romans 16, 1 Corinthians 16, Acts 18, and 2 Timothy 4. Answer the questions below.

1. What was Priscilla and Aquila's profession?

2. Why did they leave Italy and go to Corinth?

3. In which city did Paul leave Priscilla and Aquila?

4. In Ephesus, which man did they disciple?

5. In which city did Paul stay with Priscilla and Aquila?

6. In what place did Apollos teach the scriptures?

7. What were the only scriptures available at the time of Paul?

8. In 1 Corinthians 16:19, what happened on a regular basis in Priscilla and Aquila's house?

9. In Romans 16:3, what did Priscilla and Aquila do for Paul?

10. Who did Priscilla and Aquila believe was the Messiah?

SHIPWRECKED!

Read Acts 25:23-27 and 27:1-28:10. Answer the questions below.

1) Why did Paul travel to Rome?

2) Which sea did Paul sail across?

3) What was the name of the port where the ship first stopped?

4) In which place was the ship's crew planning to spend the winter?

5) Why did Paul not want to continue sailing past Yom Kippur?

6) What island was Paul shipwrecked on?

7) On the island, what came out of the fire and attacked Paul?

8) How long did Paul stay on the island?

9) What was the name of the centurion in charge of Paul?

10) Which man did Paul heal while he stayed on the island?

PETER

Read Matthew 8:14-17, 17:1-13, John 1, 13:1-36, 18, 21, and Acts 1, 5, 9, and 12. Answer the questions below.

1. What was Peter's job?

2. Whom did Peter say we ought to obey? (Acts 5:29)

3. How many times was Peter rescued by an angel from prison?

4. Which king had Peter arrested? (Acts 12:1-2)

5. How many times did Peter deny Yeshua?

6. To whom was the book of 1 Peter written?

7. What did Peter, James and John witness on a mountain with Yeshua? (Matthew 17:1)

8. What did Peter find with a coin in its mouth?

9. Which female disciple did Peter raise from the dead?

10. Peter was a disciple of which famous teacher?

Peter's prison ESCAPE

Read Acts 12:1-19. Answer the questions below.

1. Who was king of Judea at this time?

2. Which disciple had the king recently killed?

3. Peter was put in prison during which Appointed Time (Feast)?

4. How many squads of soldiers guarded Peter?

5. How was Peter bound in prison?

6. Who prayed for Peter while he was in prison?

7. How did the angel wake up Peter?

8. What did the angel say to Peter?

9. As Peter walked through the city, what opened without any help?

10. Whose house did Peter first go after escaping from prison?

Fruit of the SPIRIT

Read 1 Corinthians 13, 1 Timothy 6, Lamentations 3, Romans 12, Psalm 145, 119, Galatians 5, Nahum 1, Mark 12, and John 16. Answer the questions below.

1. Love is _____, love is kind (1 Corinthians 13:4)

2. Pursue righteousness, godliness, faith, love, steadfastness, and _____. (1 Timothy 6:11)

3. Great is your _____. (Lamentations 3:23)

4. Do the best you can to live in _____ with everyone. (Romans 12:18)

5. Yahweh is gracious, merciful, slow to anger, and of great loving _____. (Psalm 145:8)

6. Your statutes are my heritage forever; they are the _____ of my heart. (Psalm 119:111)

7. The fruit of the Spirit is love, joy, peace, patience, kindness, goodness, faithfulness, gentleness, and _____. (Galatians 5:22)

8. Yahweh is _____, A stronghold in the day of trouble. (Nahum 1:7)

9. _____ your neighbor as yourself. (Mark 12:31)

10. What is the role of the Holy Spirit? (John 16:8)

PETER & CORNELIUS

Read Acts 10:1-48. Answer the questions below.

1. In which town did Cornelius live?

2. What was Cornelius' job?

3. What did Cornelius see in a vision?

4. What instructions was Cornelius given in the vision?

5. Where was Peter staying in Joppa?

6. When Peter fell into a trance, what did he see?

7. What was the meaning of Peter's vision? (Acts 10:28)

8. What did Peter talk to Cornelius and his family about?

9. What happened while Peter was speaking to Cornelius' family?

10. What did Peter say Cornelius and his family should do?

Peter the HEALER

Read Acts 3. Answer the questions below.

1 In which city was the temple?

2 Why did Peter and John go to the temple?

3 At what time did they go to the temple?

4 What type of man was carried into the temple?

5 Where did this man used to sit and beg?

6 What did the man ask Peter and John?

7 What did Peter say to the man?

8 After Peter spoke to the man, what happened next?

9 How did the people in the temple react to the miracle?

10 What did Peter accuse the people in the temple of doing?

ANGELS

Read Genesis 32, Exodus 3, Numbers 22, Daniel 6, Jude 1, Luke 1, Judges 13, Acts 1, 5 and 12, and Revelation 8. Answer the questions below.

1. Which Bible character did an angel let out of prison? (Acts 12)

2. Which man in the Old Testament wrestled with an angel?

3. How did God protect Daniel from the lions?

4. In the Book of Revelation, how many angels are given shofars (trumpets)? (Revelation 8)

5. Where did Moses first meet the Angel of God?

6. How did the Angel of God look to Samson's mother? (Judges 13)

7. Who was the angel who appeared to Mary?

8. How many angels appeared to the disciples after Yeshua rose to Heaven?

9. Which Old Testament prophet's animal was scared when it saw the Angel of God? (Numbers 22)

10. Which angel fought Ha'Satan over the body of Moses? (Jude 1:9)

ANSWER KEY

The Creation
1. Day
2. Heaven
3. Earth
4. Sun
5. Fifth day
6. His own image
7. Seventh day (Sabbath)
8. A mist rose from the earth
9. From dust of the earth, and then breathed life into him
10. From Adam's rib

Adam & Eve
1. A mist rose from the ground
2. Eden
3. To work
4. Adam
5. She was mother of all the living
6. Eve
7. Made loincloths
8. Out of the garden
9. Cain and Abel
10. 930 years

Garden of Eden
1. Eden
2. Pishon
3. Gold
4. Bdellium and onyx stone
5. Euphrates
6. Gihon
7. Tree of the knowledge of good and evil
8. Took one of his ribs and made a woman
9. You will not surely die
10. Cherubim with a flaming sword

Cain & Abel
1. Cain
2. Farmer
3. Shepherd
4. Fruit and vegetables
5. God accepted Abel's offering but not Cain's
6. Killed him
7. Cain
8. Made him a fugitive and wanderer on the earth
9. Adam
10. Land of Nod, east of Eden

Noah's ark
1. Lamech
2. 300 cubits
3. Gopher wood
4. One
5. Seven
6. Six hundred years
7. An olive leaf
8. Mountains of Ararat
9. Altar
10. A rainbow

Tower of Babel
1. They all spoke one language
2. To the heavens
3. Brick and bitumen
4. Yahweh / God
5. He mixed their languages
6. They didn't understand one another's speech
7. Land of Shinar
8. Yahweh scattered them all over the earth
9. Being scattered
10. Modern-day Iraq

Abraham
1. Haran
2. Terah
3. Sarai (Sarah)
4. Land of Canaan
5. Fought to save him
6. Bread and wine
7. Father of the multitude
8. 100 years
9. Isaac
10. Land of Egypt

Lot's escape
1. Mamre
2. Lot was Abraham's nephew
3. Two
4. Unleavened bread
5. They were blinded
6. His sons-in-law
7. Fire and sulfur (brimstone) out of heaven
8. "Escape for your life. Do not look back or stop anywhere in the valley."
9. Turned into a pillar of salt
10. Zoar

Birth of Isaac
1. Three
2. Made them a meal
3. Sarah
4. He would have a son
5. She laughed
6. 100 years
7. Isaac
8. Eight days
9. They held a great feast
10. To offer Isaac as a burnt offering

Isaac & Rebecca
1. Abraham
2. Mesopotamia
3. Ten camels
4. By a spring
5. A gold ring and two bracelets
6. Bethuel
7. Covered herself with a veil
8. 40 years
9. The Negeb
10. Jacob and Esau

Jacob & Esau
1. Rebekah
2. Isaac
3. Nations
4. Skillful hunter and a man of the field
5. Jacob
6. A meal
7. Hunting
8. Kill Jacob
9. Jacob put on goat skins
10. Leah

Jacob
1. Rebekah
2. Land of Canaan
3. Abraham
4. Stairway / ladder
5. Leah was Jacob's first wife
6. Jacob had twelve sons
7. God changed Jacob's name to Israel
8. Joseph
9. Jacob and his family moved to the land of Egypt to live near Joseph
10. Jacob was 147 years old when he died

Joseph
1. Jacob
2. Bundles of wheat bowing down to other bundles
3. Threw him in a pit and sold him to strangers
4. Potifar
5. Butler and baker
6. Interpreted his dreams
7. To buy grain
8. Grain money and a silver cup
9. Ephraim and Manasseh
10. Land of Goshen

Moses
1. Levi
2. Pharaoh's daughter
3. Aaron
4. Land of Midian
5. From within a burning bush
6. Zipporah
7. Took care of the flocks
8. Ashes
9. Kill a lamb and brush its blood on the doorposts and lintel of their homes
10. Land of Egypt

The burning bush
1. On Mount Horeb (Sinai)
2. His shoes
3. I am the God of Abraham, Isaac, and Jacob
4. Covered his face because he was afraid
5. Lead the Israelites out of Egypt
6. Turned Moses' staff into a snake, and turned his hand leprous for a while
7. He was not a good speaker
8. His brother Aaron
9. Jethro, his father-in-law
10. Gold, silver, and fine clothing

Ten plagues of Egypt
1. Water turns into blood
2. Turning water into blood, and frogs
3. Flies
4. Boils
5. Darkness
6. Death of the firstborn
7. God sent ten plagues on the land of Egypt
8. Yahweh
9. Moses took the bones of Joseph
10. Feast of Unleavened Bread

The Passover meal
1. God sent ten plagues on the land of Egypt
2. Painted lamb's blood on the door-posts and lintel of their homes
3. Tenth day of the first month (Aviv)
4. At twilight on the 14th day of the first month (Aviv)
5. Lamb, bread, and bitter herbs
6. Unleavened bread (Matzah)
7. The Feast of Unleavened Bread
8. Throughout their generations (forever)
9. Golgotha
10. Yeshua was of the tribe of Judah

Red Sea crossing
1. Moses
2. Weapons, the Egyptians' jewelry, and the bones of Joseph
3. The Angel of God in a pillar of cloud or fire
4. The Egyptian army
5. Pi Hahiroth, between Migdol and the sea, opposite Baal Zephon
6. He lifted up his rod and stretched his hand over the sea
7. Red Sea
8. He made the wheels of their chariots break
9. They drowned in the sea
10. Sang a song to Yah

The ten commandments
1. Moses and the Israelites
2. Honor your father and mother
3. 6th commandment
4. Two tablets of stone
5. Remember the Sabbath
6. 9th commandment
7. 8th commandment
8. 2nd commandment
9. Mount Sinai
10. Do not desire your neighbor's possessions

The golden calf
1. Made a golden calf
2. Gold
3. Offered burnt offerings and peace offerings
4. Threatened to destroy the Israelites
5. Smashed two stone tablets on the ground
6. Melted it in the fire and ground it to dust
7. Aaron
8. He forced them to drink gold dust
9. God sent a plague
10. Base of Mount Sinai

The tabernacle
1. Aaron was the first high priest
2. For God to dwell among His people Israel
3. On top of the ark of the covenant
4. Pure gold
5. Priests were chosen from the tribe of Levi
6. Bezaleel and Aholiab
7. Book of Exodus
8. Pure olive oil
9. To burn offerings and sacrifices
10. The ark of the covenant was made of acacia wood

Korah rebels
1. Levi
2. Izhar
3. 250 men
4. Moses and Aaron
5. Fell on his face
6. Take censers and put fire in them and incense on them, and stand before God
7. The tents of Korah, Dathan, and Abiram
8. Swallowed up the men and their households
9. Plague
10. Moses

Joshua
1. Moses
2. Under stalks of flax
3. The walls fells down
4. Jordan River
5. Set up 12 stones, one for each of the tribes of Israel
6. Tribes of Israel
7. A whole day
8. Gibeonites
9. Hailstones
10. 110 years

Twelve spies in Canaan
1. Twelve tribes
2. Desert of Paran
3. Twelve spies
4. Through the Negev
5. Fruit
6. Giants (Nephilim)
7. Amalekites
8. Forty days
9. Grapes, pomegranates, and figs
10. Caleb and Joshua

Balaam's donkey
1. Twelve tribes of Israel
2. King Balak
3. To curse the Israelites
4. Two servants
5. Numbers 22-25
6. A donkey spoke to Balaam
7. Balaam traveled to Moab and blessed the Israelites
8. Balaam blessed the Israelites three times
9. Send the Moabite women to party with the Israelites (Numbers 31:15)
10. One thousand men from each tribe

Rahab and the spies
1. Joshua
2. Shittim
3. The Bible does not say
4. In the city wall
5. Under flax on the roof of her house
6. King of Jericho
7. Jordan River
8. Used a rope to help the men escape through a window
9. Because she hid the spies
10. Scarlet thread

Gideon
1. The Israelites did evil before God
2. In a winepress
3. Save the Israelites from the Midianites
4. Meat and unleavened cakes
5. Altar of Baal
6. Fleece
7. 32,000 from Asher, Zebulun, Naphtali, and Manasseh
8. 300 men
9. Shofars and jars with torches inside
10. Locust

Ruth & Boaz
1. Land of Moab
2. Orpah
3. Mahlon
4. Naomi
5. Boaz's field
6. Bread and roasted grain
7. At Boaz's feet
8. Six measures of barley
9. Judah
10. Obed

Samson
1. Angel of God
2. Don't drink wine or eat anything unclean, or cut Samson's hair
3. A lion
4. Samson's bride told them
5. 300 foxes
6. 1000
7. Twenty years
8. 1,100 pieces of silver
9. He became weak
10. The temple of Dagon

Samson & Delilah
1. Nazarite
2. Twenty years
3. 1,100 pieces of silver from each Philistine chief
4. Philistine
5. Valley of Sorek
6. Seven fresh bowstrings
7. New ropes
8. Seven locks of Samson's hair
9. "If my head is shaved, then my strength will leave me…" (Judges 16)
10. With bronze shackles

Samuel
1. Eli, the priest
2. A robe
3. His mother had dedicated him to God (a Nazarite vow)
4. A king
5. Make them servants, tax them, and take their sons to be soldiers
6. Saul
7. Levi
8. Joel and Abijah
9. Saul and his sons will die in battle
10. Sheol, where he sleeps

King Saul
1. Benjamin
2. Philistines
3. Samuel
4. Kish
5. Jonathan
6. Samuel
7. David
8. Played his harp for King Saul
9. Witch of Endor
10. Battle at Mount Giboa

Witch of Endor
1. Israelites
2. Philistines
3. To understand the future
4. Endor
5. The prophet Samuel
6. To learn how to defeat the Philistines
7. Saul and his sons will lose their lives
8. Went into battle against the Philistines
9. Deuteronomy 18
10. Fell on his sword

Ark is captured
1. Philistines
2. Ebenezer
3. 30,000 Israelites
4. Eli's sons (Hophni and Phinehas)
5. Fell over backwards and died
6. Statue of Dagon
7. It fell face downward to the ground
8. Tumors
9. Seven months
10. The Philistines put the ark on a cart pulled by two milk cows

David & Goliath
1. Shepherd
2. The prophet Samuel
3. Harp / Lyre
4. Valley of Elah
5. About 9 feet 9 inches
6. Forty
7. King Saul
8. Five stones
9. He hit him with a stone from his sling
10. Singing and dancing, and playing instruments

Kings of the Bible
1. Saul
2. Samuel
3. Darius
4. Balak
5. Solomon
6. Shepherd
7. Belshazzar
8. Ahasuerus
9. Nebuchadnezzar
10. Herod the Tetrarch

People of the Torah
1. Balaam
2. Rebekah
3. 600 years
4. Joseph
5. Moses
6. Lamech
7. Joshua
8. Aaron
9. Abraham
10. Jacob

King Solomon
1. King David
2. Zadok
3. Gihon
4. The gift of wisdom
5. Seven years
6. Hiram, king of Tyre
7. Spices, gold, and precious stones
8. 700 wives
9. Forty years
10. Jeroboam

Queen of Sheba
1. To test Solomon with difficult questions
2. Camels carrying spices, gold and precious stones
3. Happy
4. Solomon's palace, servants, food, his wisdom, and temple offerings
5. Blessed be Adonai, your God.
6. Jerusalem
7. Bathsheba
8. Make pillars for the temple and palace, and musical instruments
9. Everything she desired
10. The queen and her servants returned home

Hezekiah's gold
1. 25 years old
2. Ahaz
3. Sennacherib
4. Isaiah
5. Jerusalem
6. Three hundred talents of silver and thirty talents of gold
7. Gold
8. The Temple
9. The Angel of God
10. God's commandments

Isaiah

1. Prophet
2. Amoz
3. Scarlet and crimson
4. You will live another 15 years, and God will deliver you and the city from the Assyrians
5. Two children; Maher-shalal-hash-baz and Shear-jashub
6. The Israelites
7. Four kings; Uzziah, Jotham, Ahaz, and Hezekiah
8. Tribe of Judah
9. Everything will be taken away to Babylon
10. Sixty-six chapters

False prophets of Baal

1. Three
2. 850
3. Mount Carmel
4. Danced around the altar
5. Lighting a fire under the sacrifice on the altar
6. Bull
7. Water, stones, soil and sacrifice
8. One stone for each tribe of Israel
9. Four
10. Fell on their faces

Josiah and the Torah

1. Eight years
2. Amon
3. Timber and stone
4. Hilkiah the High Priest
5. Shaphan
6. He tore his clothes
7. Incense altars, altars of the Baals, and Asherah poles
8. The Passover meal
9. The people joined in the covenant
10. At the brook Kidron

King Nebuchadnezzar

1. Babylon
2. Belteshazzar
3. Jehoiakim
4. The king made Daniel ruler over the province of Babylon and chief of all the Magi
5. Kingdoms of the world
6. Ninety feet tall and nine feet wide
7. Plain of Dura
8. Shadrach, Meshach and Abednego
9. Threw them into a fiery furnace
10. The Angel of God

The fiery furnace

1. Babylonia
2. Shadrach, Meshach and Abednego
3. King Nebuchadnezzar
4. The Hebrew men refused to worship the king's golden statue
5. The king had the three Hebrew men thrown into a furnace
6. The furnace was seven times hotter
7. The flame of the fire killed those men who threw Shadrach, Meshach, and Abednego into the furnace
8. The king saw four men walking about safely in the fire
9. The men were given more important jobs
10. Shadrach, Meshach and Abednego' hair was not singed, their clothes had not changed, and they did not smell of smoke

Daniel and the lions

1. Belteshazzar
2. Interpret his dreams
3. Pulses and water
4. A group of Magi
5. Thrown into the lions' den
6. For praying to Yah, the god of Abraham, Isaac and Jacob
7. Darius
8. With a large stone
9. An angel of God shut the lion's mouths
10. Thrown into the lions' den

Jonah and the big fish

1. Nineveh
2. Tarshish
3. Joppa
4. Sailors
5. He was swallowed by a big fish
6. Three days and three nights
7. To repent
8. Put on sackcloth and fasted
9. Went out of the city and made a shelter
10. A worm attacked the plant

Nehemiah

1. Kingdom of Persia
2. Cup-bearer to the king of Persia
3. From Hanani and certain men of Judah
4. Nehemiah asked the king of Persia for permission to return to Jerusalem and rebuild the city walls
5. They accused Nehemiah of turning against the king
6. Eliashib was the high priest
7. The priests
8. It took the Israelites 52 days to rebuild the walls
9. The Israelites' enemies lost their courage because they knew God had helped the Israelites rebuild the walls
10. Feast of Sukkot (Tabernacles)

Esther saves her people
1. King Ahasuerus (Xerxes)
2. Esther (Hadassah)
3. Queen Vashti
4. So the king would hang Mordecai on them
5. Do not tell anyone you are a Hebrew, or who I am
6. Fast (not eat for a period of time)
7. Held out his golden scepter
8. The king & Haman
9. Haman
10. Sent letters throughout Persia allowing the Hebrews to defend themselves

The story of Job
1. Uz
2. Ten children (seven sons, three daughters)
3. A house fell on them
4. "Have you considered My servant, Job; there is none like him on the earth."
5. Job's wife
6. Seven days and seven nights
7. Money and a ring of gold
8. Out of a whirlwind
9. In the sea
10. Gave him twice as much as he had before

Twelve tribes of Israel
1. Ephraim
2. 48
3. Benjamin
4. Manasseh
5. Levi
6. Levi
7. Dan, Asher, Naphtali
8. Ephraim and Manasseh
9. Reuben and Gad, and half of Manasseh
10. The twelve tribes scattered abroad

Women of the Bible
1. Daughter-in-law
2. Rebekah
3. Miriam
4. Lydia
5. Bathsheba
6. Esther
7. Mary
8. Uncovered his feet and lay down next to him
9. Deborah
10. Elizabeth

Mothers of the Bible
1. Rebekah
2. Sarai (Sarah)
3. Rachel
4. Rebekah
5. Eve
6. Mary
7. Deborah (Judges 5:7)
8. Bathsheba
9. Moses' mother
10. Hagar

Fathers of the Bible
1. Terah
2. Father of the prodigal son
3. Jairus
4. Rachel
5. Greek
6. Zechariah
7. David
8. Isaac
9. The fifth commandment
10. Jesse

John the Baptist
1. Elizabeth
2. Zacharias
3. Jordan
4. Judea
5. Yeshua
6. Galilee
7. Camel hair
8. Locusts
9. Behold, the lamb of God, who takes away the sin of the world!
10. Herod Antipas

An angel visits Mary
1. Nazareth
2. The sixth month
3. Gabriel
4. Joseph
5. Greetings, O favored one, God is with you!
6. She was troubled and afraid
7. She will get pregnant and give birth to the Son of God
8. Yeshua
9. Mary was a virgin
10. Through the power of the Holy Spirit

Birth of the Messiah

1. Yeshua
2. Emperor Augustus
3. They were descendants of David from Bethlehem
4. Bethlehem
5. Herod (the great)
6. Judah (Mat 1:1)
7. He would be born in Bethlehem
8. The Bible doesn't say
9. Gave orders to kill every boy in Bethlehem under two years old
10. The land of Egypt

The shepherd's visit

1. Taking care of their flocks
2. An Angel of God
3. They were afraid
4. Today in Bethlehem was born a Deliverer who is the Messiah
5. A baby wrapped in cloth and lying in a feeding trough
6. Bethlehem
7. Mary and Joseph, and the baby lying in the feeding trough
8. Everything the angel had told them about the child
9. Yeshua
10. Returned to their flocks, glorifying and praising God

The Magi

1. King Herod
2. They saw a bright star in the sky
3. The newborn King of the Judeans
4. Bethlehem
5. Bowed down and worshipped Him
6. The Bible doesn't say
7. Gold, frankincense and myrrh
8. The Magi were warned in a dream not to visit Herod again
9. The book of Daniel
10. Ordered the deaths of all boys in Bethlehem under two years old

Presentation in the temple

1. The angel Gabriel
2. Jerusalem
3. The eighth day
4. To be purified, as was written in the Torah
5. Simeon
6. Fasted & prayed
7. Eight four years
8. Asher
9. A pair of turtledoves, or two young pigeons
10. To their hometown of Nazareth

The twelve disciples

1. Matthew
2. Simon (Peter) & Andrew
3. Peter
4. Philip, Andrew, and Peter
5. Transfiguration
6. Donkey and colt
7. Judas
8. He washed their feet
9. John
10. Matthias

The temple

1. Solomon
2. He was a man of war (1 Chr 28:3)
3. Jerusalem
4. Holy of Holies
5. Day of Atonement (Lev 16)
6. Solomon's porch
7. Twice (John 3 & Mat 21)
8. At least 46 years (John 2)
9. The Feasts of Unleavened Bread, Pentecost, and Tabernacles
10. The Israelites

Wedding feast at Cana

1. A wedding
2. Cana
3. Mary
4. Yeshua's disciples
5. Six stone jars
6. Thirty gallons
7. Water
8. Wine
9. The bridegroom
10. Capernaum

Capernaum

1. Fishing village
2. Simon (Peter)
3. Andrew, Peter, James, John
4. Sea of Galilee
5. The servant of a Roman centurion
6. Inside a fish's mouth
7. Through the roof
8. The Sabbath
9. Simon Peter
10. He had the spirit of an unclean demon

Tempted in the wilderness
1. The Spirit
2. The Adversary (Devil)
3. Forty days and nights
4. When he was hungry
5. Three times
6. Stones
7. Temple roof
8. Kingdoms of the Word
9. Deuteronomy
10. Angels came and took care of Yeshua

Sermon on the mount
1. His disciples
2. Your reward in Heaven is great
3. The meek
4. Moths and rust destroy it, and thieves steal it
5. Do for them more than they expect you to do (go the extra mile)
6. Treat others as we would like them to treat us
7. Seek first his Kingdom and his righteousness
8. Their lives – what they will eat, drink, and wear
9. In private (in their rooms)
10. The Torah (Law)

Feeding the 5000
1. Two fish and five barley loaves.
2. 5000 men, plus women and children
3. Lake Tiberius
4. On a hill near Lake Galilee
5. To test Philip
6. He blessed the bread
7. Twelve baskets
8. Galilee
9. The Feast of Unleavened Bread
10. To a mountain by Himself to pray

Jairus' daughter
1. A synagogue official named Jairus
2. believe (Mark 5:36)
3. Peter, James, and John
4. Weeping and wailing
5. Twelve years
6. Because Yeshua told them the girl was not dead but sleeping
7. "Little girl, get up!"
8. She got up and began walking
9. Galilee
10. To feed the girl, and not tell anyone what He had done

Zacchaeus the tax collector
1. Tax collector
2. Rich
3. Jericho
4. Zacchaeus' house
5. Because he was short and couldn't see Yeshua
6. Sycamore
7. Judah
8. The lost sheep of the House of Israel
9. Half of his goods
10. Fourfold

Parable of the talents
1. Five talents
2. Two talents
3. One talent
4. Traded with them and made five more talents
5. Gained two more talents
6. Dug a hole in the ground and buried his talent
7. Well done, good and faithful servants, You have been faithful over a little; I will put you in charge of much.
8. I was afraid and hid your talent in the ground
9. He became angry
10. Took the talent and gave it to the servant who had ten talents

Parable of the wise & foolish virgins
1. Ten
2. Five
3. The virgins all slept
4. Midnight
5. Go out to meet the bridegroom
6. Lamps with no oil
7. Lamps full of oil
8. Give us some of your oil for our lamps are going out
9. The bridegroom arrived and went into the wedding with the wise virgins, and shut the door
10. He said He did not know them

Parable of the good Samaritan
1. To Jericho
2. He was robbed and beaten
3. A priest
4. A Levite
5. A Samaritan
6. Cleaned his wounds and paid an innkeeper to take care of him
7. Two denarii
8. A Torah teacher
9. "You shall love God with all your heart, soul, and strength; and your neighbor as yourself." (Deuteronomy 6:5)
10. "He who showed mercy on him."

Parable of the prodigal son

1. Two sons
2. Youngest son
3. A far away country
4. There was a famine
5. Feeding pigs
6. He came to his senses (repentance)
7. The eldest son
8. Ran to his son, threw his arms around him and kissed him
9. Good shoes, clothes and a ring
10. Killed a fatted calf and had a party

Woman at the well

1. He learned the Pharisees had heard He was making and baptizing more disciples than John
2. Galilee
3. Jacob's well
4. Samaria
5. Into Sychar to buy food
6. Five
7. spirit
8. Himself
9. drinks
10. Because of this woman's testimony

The transfiguration

1. Peter, James, and John
2. Sleepy
3. They became intensely white (radiant)
4. Moses and Elijah
5. Make three shelters (sukkahs)
6. Yeshua's departure that would soon take place in Jerusalem
7. A cloud
8. This is My Son, my Chosen One, listen to Him!
9. Yahweh
10. The next day

Triumphal entry

1. Feast of Unleavened Bread
2. Galilee
3. Bethpage
4. Two disciples
5. Yeshua
6. They spread cloaks and branches from trees on the road
7. "Blessed is he who comes in the name of the Lord! Hosanna in the highest!"
8. The temple
9. The Passover meal
10. Zechariah (Zechariah 9:9)

Yeshua clears the temple

1. His disciples
2. Selling animals and changing money
3. Rope / cord
4. Jerusalem
5. Turning the temple into a den of robbers
6. Oxen, doves, pigeons, and sheep
7. Poured out their money and overturned the tables
8. King Herod
9. House of prayer
10. Feast of Unleavened Bread

Judas

1. Disciples
2. Bread
3. The religious leaders (chief priests)
4. 30 pieces of silver
5. Garden of Gethsemane
6. With a kiss
7. Master
8. Akeldama (Field of Blood)
9. Joseph and Matthias
10. Matthias

The last supper

1. Jerusalem
2. Feast of Unleavened Bread
3. Twelve
4. Peter
5. Bread and wine
6. "This is My body which is given for you; do this to remember Me."
7. Love one another; as I have loved you. (John 13)
8. Which of them should be considered the greatest
9. Judas
10. Garden of Gethsemane

Gethsemane

1. Garden of Gethsemane
2. They fell asleep
3. Watch and pray so that you will not fall into temptation.
4. Peter
5. With a kiss
6. An angel
7. Soldiers and Temple guards
8. Peter
9. They left Yeshua and ran away
10. To meet Annas, and then Caiaphas

Armor of God

1. peace
2. righteousness
3. truth
4. flesh
5. armor
6. feet
7. helmet
8. perseverance
9. strong
10. sword

Yeshua before Pilate

1. Only the Romans could put someone to death
2. Chief priests and elders
3. Judgment Hall
4. Telling people to disobey the Romans, not to pay taxes to Caesar, and that He says He is a king
5. Yeshua didn't answer them (He remained silent)
6. Herod Antipas
7. Crucify Him
8. Barabbas
9. Pilate's wife
10. To show that Yeshua was innocent and that he wanted no part in His death

Death on the stake

1. Pilate, the Roman Governor
2. Simon of Cyrene
3. Golgotha
4. King of the Judeans
5. My God, my God, why have you forsaken me?
6. Two criminals
7. Three hours
8. Joseph of Arimathea
9. Spear
10. Linen cloth

The resurrection

1. An angel
2. First Fruits, during the week of Unleavened Bread
3. Money
4. Mary Magdalene
5. An empty tomb
6. "Why do you seek the living among the dead? He is not here, but has risen."
7. Thomas
8. Sea of Galilee
9. 40 days (Acts 1:3)
10. Go and make disciples

Road to Emmaus

1. The Feast of Unleavened Bread
2. Two disciples (Cleopas and one other man)
3. Seven miles
4. Yeshua
5. A man who was a prophet mighty in deed and word before God and all the people
6. A vision of angels
7. Moses and the Prophets (Old Testament)
8. Invited the stranger to eat with them
9. After Yeshua made a blessing and broke bread
10. Yeshua disappeared from their sight

The ascension

1. Forty days
2. Sea of Galilee
3. Peter
4. Do you love Me?
5. The Holy Spirit (Ruach HaKodesh)
6. Judea, Samaria and to many other countries
7. Mount of Olives
8. A cloud
9. Two men dressed in white
10. Yeshua will return to you the same way He left

Feast of Pentecost

1. Mount Sinai
2. Forty days and nights
3. Twelve tribes of Israel
4. The 4th commandment
5. Honor your father and mother
6. A sound from heaven like rushing wind
7. Each person heard the disciples speaking to them in their own language
8. Peter
9. About three thousand people
10. Jerusalem

Feast of Tabernacles

1. Forever – throughout the generations
2. Seven days, plus the Last Great Day
3. Sukkot (Tabernacles)
4. On the fifteenth day of the seventh month
5. Live in temporary dwellings and rejoice (a wedding celebration!)
6. Fall (Northern hemisphere), Spring (Southern hemisphere)
7. First and eighth day
8. The Israelite's exodus out of the land of Egypt
9. King Solomon
10. No rain

Philip and the Ethiopian
1. Get ready and go south on the road that leads to Gaza from Jerusalem
2. A man from Ethiopia
3. To worship God
4. A court official of Candace, queen of the Ethiopians
5. A chariot
6. Go to that chariot and stay near it
7. Isaiah the prophet
8. Yeshua the Messiah
9. Immerse himself in the water
10. The Spirit of God carried Philip away

Road to Damascus
1. Tarsus
2. Paul (Sha'ul)
3. To find and arrest disciples of Yeshua
4. High Priest
5. A light from heaven
6. Yeshua
7. Three days
8. Ananias
9. Yeshua is the Messiah
10. In a basket down the city wall

Paul's letters
1. honor
2. persecute
3. love
4. transformed
5. spirit
6. thanks
7. commandment, neighbor
8. nothing
9. Law (Torah)
10. imitators

Paul before King Agrippa
1. Caesarea
2. Yeshua the Messiah
3. Festus
4. Bernice
5. Chief priests in Jerusalem
6. Pharisee
7. Caesar
8. Felix
9. Chains
10. Paul told them to repent and turn back to God's Ways

Priscilla & Aquila
1. Tent-makers
2. Claudius ordered all Jews to leave Rome
3. Ephesus
4. Apollos
5. Corinth
6. In a synagogue
7. Old Testament (Tanakh)
8. People gathered together
9. Risked their lives for him
10. Yeshua

Shipwrecked!
1. To meet the Roman Emperor and plead his case
2. Mediterranean Sea
3. Sidon
4. Phoenix
5. Bad weather
6. Malta
7. A viper (snake)
8. Three months
9. Julius
10. The father of Publius

Peter
1. Fisherman
2. God
3. Two times
4. King Herod
5. Three times
6. Lost sheep of the House of Israel
7. Transfiguration
8. A fish
9. Tabitha
10. Yeshua

Peter's prison escape
1. King Herod
2. James, the brother of John
3. Feast of Unleavened Bread
4. Four
5. In chains
6. The Church
7. An angel struck Peter on his side
8. "Wrap your cloak around you and follow me."
9. Iron gates into the city
10. Mary, mother of John

Fruit of the Spirit

1. Patient
2. Gentleness
3. Faithfulness
4. Peace
5. Kindness
6. Joy
7. Self-control
8. Good
9. Love
10. Conviction of sin, instruction in righteousness, and sound judgment

Peter & Cornelius

1. Caesarea
2. Roman centurion
3. An angel of God
4. Send men to Joppa and get Peter
5. At the house of Simon the tanner
6. A container like a big sheet being lowered to the ground by its four corners. In it were all kinds of animals, reptiles, and birds.
7. God showed Peter that no man should call any person clean or unclean (at that time it was unlawful for a Jew to spend time with non-Jewish people)
8. Yeshua the Messiah
9. The Holy Spirit fell on everyone who heard the message
10. Be baptized (immersed) in the name of Yeshua the Messiah

Peter the healer

1. Jerusalem
2. To pray
3. Ninth hour
4. A crippled man
5. Beautiful Gate
6. For money
7. "I don't have money but in the name of Yeshua, walk!"
8. The man stood up and walked into the Temple
9. Full of amazement, they ran toward Peter and John in Solomon's Colonnade
10. Killing Yeshua and freeing Barabbas

Angels

1. Peter
2. Jacob (Israel)
3. An angel of God shut the lion's mouths
4. Seven
5. In a burning bush on Mount Sinai
6. Fearsome
7. Gabriel
8. Two
9. His donkey
10. The archangel Michael

◈ DISCOVER MORE ACTIVITY BOOKS! ◈

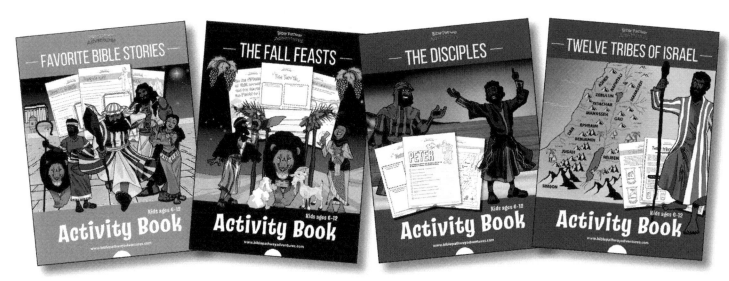

Available for purchase at www.biblepathwayadventures.com

Made in the USA
Columbia, SC
28 December 2022

75126670R00067